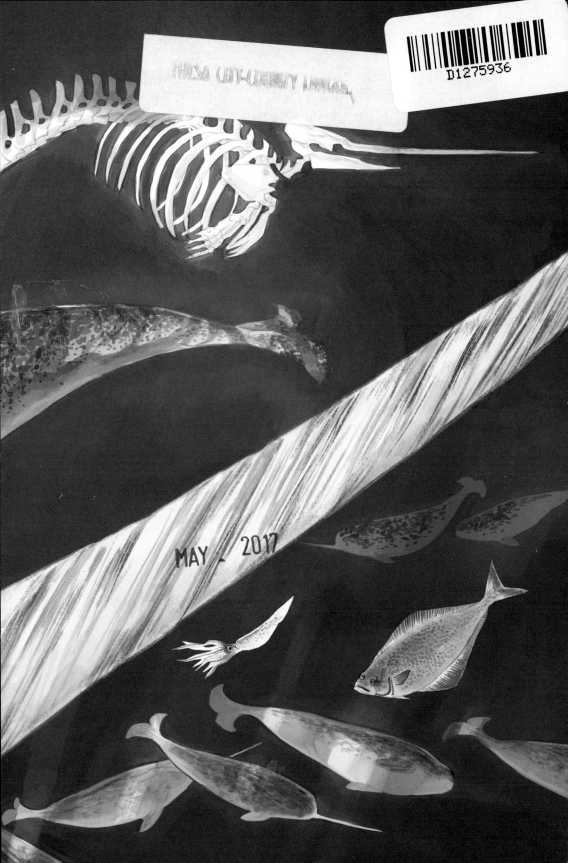

D1275936

·ANIMALS ILLUSTRATED·

Narwhal

·ANIMALS ILLUSTRATED·
Narwhal

by Solomon Awa • illustrated by Hwei Lim

INHABIT
MEDIA

Published by Inhabit Media Inc.
www.inhabitmedia.com

Inhabit Media Inc. (Iqaluit), P.O. Box 11125, Iqaluit, Nunavut, X0A 1H0 · (Toronto), 191 Eglinton Avenue East, Suite 301, Toronto, Ontario, M4P 1K1

Design and layout copyright © 2016 Inhabit Media Inc.
Text copyright © 2016 by Solomon Awa
Illustrations by Hwei Lim copyright © 2016 Inhabit Media Inc.

Editors: Neil Christopher, Kelly Ward
Art Director: Danny Christopher

We acknowledge the support of the Canada Council for the Arts for our publishing program.

We acknowledge the financial support of the Government of Canada through the Department of Canadian Heritage Canada Book Fund.

978-1-77227-080-8

Printed in Canada

Library and Archives Canada Cataloguing in Publication

Awa, Solomon, 1959-, author
Narwhal / by Solomon Awa ; illustrated by Hwei Lim.

(Animals illustrated)
ISBN 978-1-77227-080-8 (hardback)

1. Narwhal--Arctic regions--Juvenile literature. I. Lim, Hwei (Illustrator), illustrator II. Title. III. Series: Animals Illustrated

QL737.C433A93 2016   j599.5'43   C2016-904106-9

Table of Contents

2   The Narwhal

4   Range

8   Skeleton

10 Tusks

12 Diet

14 Babies

16 Predators

18 Under the Ice

20 Deep-Diving Whales

The Narwhal

Narwhals are medium-sized whales that live in the
Arctic all year round. They can weigh between 1,700
and 3,500 pounds (771 to 1587 kilograms), and they
can grow to 18 feet in length (about 5.5 metres). Like
all whales, narwhals are mammals. This means they
breathe air. Each narwhal has a blowhole on the top of
its head that it breathes through.

Narwhals looks different from all other whales because the males have a long tusk that looks like a long horn. Narwhals are usually black with white spots and lighter colouring on their bellies.

Let's learn more about narwhals!

Range

Narwhals live in the Arctic all year. They do
not travel to other oceans in the winter, like
many other whales do.

Narwhals usually travel in groups of about 10 to 20 whales. A group of narwhals is called a "pod." In the winter they live in very deep water that is covered in ice. In the spring, narwhals start to move toward land, and by the summer they live in shallower water closer to land.

Narwhals are most active in the summer. In the summertime they can travel in groups of hundreds of whales.

There are places in the Arctic where larger numbers of narwhals tend to live. The northwestern part of Baffin Island has many narwhals.

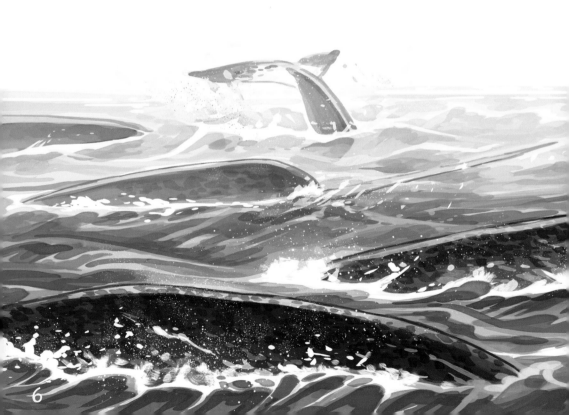

Narwhal pod seen
from above.

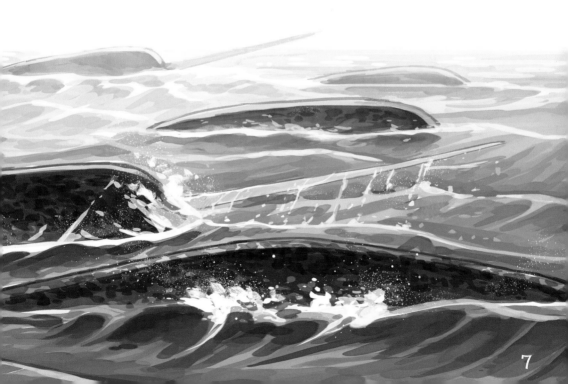

Skeleton

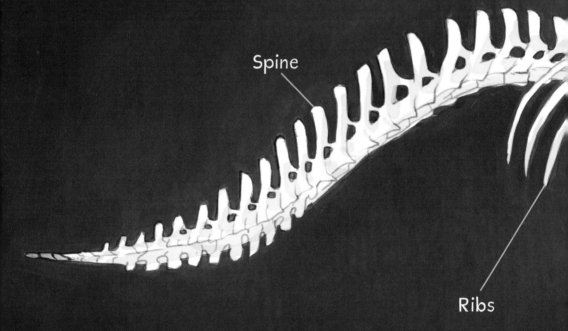

Spine

Ribs

The bones of the narwhal's
pectoral fins look a lot like
the bones of a hand.

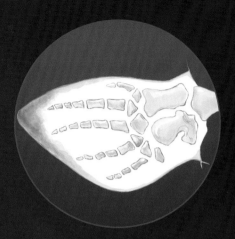

Skull

Tusk

Pectoral fins

Tusks

The narwhal's tusk is actually a very large tooth that grows out of the mouth of the male narwhal. These teeth can be huge! They can grow to be up to 9 feet (close to 3 metres) in length. Most male narwhals will have one tusk. Narwhals can have two tusks, but that is very rare.

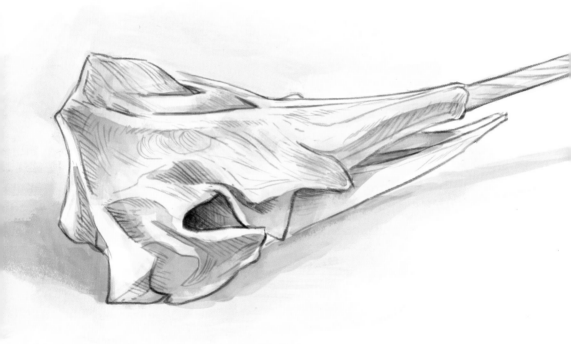

Even though the tusk is a tooth, narwhals do not use their tusks to eat. Some people think that a narwhal's tusk can sense changes in the water around the narwhal.

People are still studying the narwhal to find out all the things its tusk can do!

Diet

Narwhals mostly eat Arctic cod and halibut, and they will sometimes eat squid and shrimp.

Narwhals have only two teeth. They use their mouths to suck up their prey as it swims by.

Arctic cod

Squid
close-up

Squid

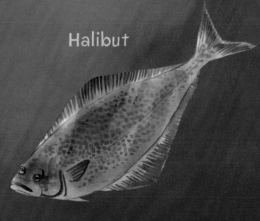

Halibut

Babies

A narwhal baby is called a "calf." Calves are born in the summer. Usually only one calf will be born at a time. Narwhal calves can swim as soon as they are born.

Narwhal calves are grey when they are born, and they turn black as they get older. Babies need to stay with their mothers for almost two years.

Predators

Narwhals are very strong, but they can still be caught by predators, which are animals that want to eat them. Orcas are one of the narwhal's main predators. Orcas chase groups of narwhals into shallow water in order to hunt them. Sometimes narwhals will come so close to the shore trying to get away from orcas that people can see narwhal pods from the shoreline.

Polar bears also like to hunt narwhals. Narwhals can sometimes become trapped in one spot if the ice shifts. When this happens, it is easy for polar bears to hunt the trapped narwhals from on top of the ice.

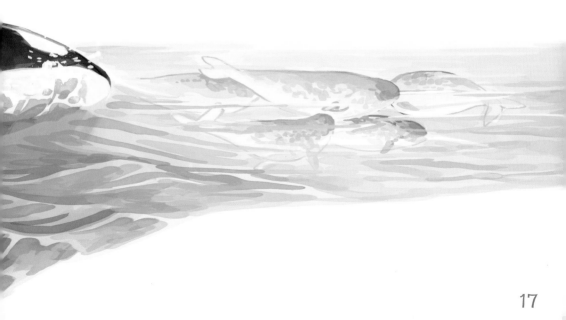

Under the ice

Narwhals spend a lot of time under the sea ice during the cold months. Because they breathe air, narwhals have to rely on narrow openings in the ice to breathe.

Deep-Diving Whales

Narwhals can dive deeper than almost any other whale. They have been known to reach depths of more than 4,900 feet (1,500 metres) on a dive. These deep dives last close to half an hour. The blood of a narwhal is able to hold a lot of oxygen for these deep dives. Narwhals have streamlined bodies that make them great divers. At these depths there is almost no light.

Solomon Awa was born in a sod house near Igloolik, Nunavut, on November 2, 1959. From a young age, he was curious about everything around him. He learned to sew traditional items such as sealskins from his late mother, Appia Awa. His late father, Mathias Awa, was an excellent carver, especially with ivory—once he made a harpoon from caribou antlers in one night—and Solomon learned to carve from him. Solomon loves to tell the stories that he learned from his father. He does this at schools, and also had the opportunity to go to Kautokeino, Norway, to tell some of these stories. He teaches traditional knowledge at Nunavut Arctic College and works for the Qikiqtani Inuit Association.

Hwei Lim studied engineering, worked in IT and business consulting, and now draws comics and other stories. Recent published works include art for *The Spirit of the Sea, Spera: Volume 1*, and the Boris & Lalage story series. Hwei lives in Malaysia.

www.inhabitmedia.com